# How to Witness to

# Shari S. Abbott

*For whosoever shall call upon the name of the Lord shall be saved. How then shall they call on him in whom they have not believed? and how shall they believe in him of whom they have not heard? and how shall they hear without a preacher? And how shall they preach, except they be sent? as it is written, How beautiful are the feet of them that preach the gospel of peace, and bring glad tidings of good things!*

*— Romans 10:13-15*

# How to Witness to Jehovah's Witnesses

Psalm267
Publishing
psalm267.com

*That I may publish with the voice of thanksgiving,
and tell of all thy wondrous works. (Psalm 26:7)*

www.psalm267.com, info@psalm267.com

© 2015 by Shari S. Abbott.

Scripture quotations are from The King James Bible, © United Kingdom Crown

Verses marked (NWT) are from the New World Translation, © 1950 (NT), 1961, 1970, 1981, 1984, 2013 Watch Tower Bible and Tract Society of Pennsylvania, www.jw.org.

All emphasis and bracketed information on Bible verses is from the author.

Printed in the United States of America
ISBN: 978-0-9885513-7-4

# Contents

*All truth is given by revelation, either general or special, and it must be received by reason. Reason is the God-given means for discovering the truth that God discloses, whether in his world or his Word. While God wants to reach the heart with truth, he does not bypass the mind.* — *Jonathan Edwards*

# Prepare to Witness

## Do not be out-witnessed by a Jehovah's Witness!

Jehovah's Witnesses (and Mormons) are dedicated to sharing their faith. They go into neighborhoods, in pairs, and share their beliefs with anyone who will listen. It's not surprising that they always witness in pairs. The Old Testament law required at least two witnesses for valid testimony (Deuteronomy 19:15). However, even with two witnesses, the testimony of Jehovah's Witnesses is not valid.

So how do we witness to Jehovah's Witnesses? Simple...We need to be prepared. We need to be willing. And we need to be confident!

Jehovah's Witnesses know what they believe, and they actively share their faith. They will come to your door very prepared, albeit with an incorrect knowledge of the King James Bible and with their own New World Translation (NWT)—an inaccurate translation of biblical manuscripts (for more information, see Appendix).

How do we prepare? Start by knowing what the Bible says. Study God's Word and know His truths. You can't present the truth, or defend God's Word, if you don't have an adequate knowledge of the Bible.

Make prayer an important part of your life. Spend time with God and seek the Holy Spirit's direction. Jesus has promised that the Spirit will teach us all things (John 14:26) and guide us in His ways (John 16:13).

### Biblical Knowledge + Prayer = Confidence to Share

While it's of utmost importance to know what our Bible teaches, it's also important to be prepared with a general knowledge of what Jehovah's Witnesses believe. As a real-life illustration, I'll share with you an encounter I had and then provide some of the most common false teachings of the Jehovah's Witnesses religion.

**Opening the Door to a Conversation of Spiritual Importance**

One bright, sunny, summer morning, I answered the door and immediately knew that the two men standing before me were Jehovah's Witnesses. Mormons are always dressed in white shirts and dark pants. The two men at my door were dressed more casual.

Just like Jehovah's Witnesses, Mormons go door-to-door in pairs. However, in my experience, Mormon who witness have always been young men. Jehovah's Witnesses send out both men and women and always there's an elder and a younger "witness." The elder seems to be experienced and knowledgeable, and the younger seems to be a trainee.

I greeted the two men. They introduced themselves and gave me a tract. I told them I was a Christian and we began a conversation. Always remember that a witnessing encounter should not be a *presentation*...it should be a *conversation*.

**Be Prepared:  Pray**

When I opened the door and saw the two men, I mentally prayed, asking the Holy Spirit to work through me to speak God's truth in love. That should be the first step in any witness encounter. We cannot effectively witness in our own strength. On that day I was particularly weak and distressed because of a personal issue, and I knew that I needed God's strength. I knew that I needed the Holy Spirit to give me words to speak and I believed that He would.

**Be Prepared: Knowledge and Sharing**

We talked for about 35-40 minutes, each of us explaining our understanding of the Bible. I have a basic knowledge of what Jehovah's Witnesses believe, so I was able to counter and challenge their theological statements that were contrary to what the Christian Bible teaches. I'll give you some examples, but first know this...

Jehovah's Witnesses believe Jesus is a created being. They believe God created Jesus and then Jesus created everything else. They do not believe that Jesus is God. They use the King James Bible and their own translation, the New World Translation. Because I know that the New World Translation is filled with additions and false translation, I told the two men that I would only discuss verses from the King James Bible (KJV). The reason I gave is that the KJV is common to both our faiths. They agreed, however both were carrying the New World Translation (NWT).

I began by bringing up John 1:1, in the KJV, knowing that the NWT adds a word to this verse.

> *(KJV) John 1:1 In the beginning was the Word, and the Word was with God, and the Word was God.*

> *(NWT) In the beginning was the Word, and the Word was with God, and the Word was **a** god.*

Jehovah's Witnesses claim that the word "a" is missing in the KJV and other translations. They insist that because the Greek language does not have indefinite articles (a, an) it was not present in the original language, but it should be added in the English translations. This reasoning does not justify inserting the word "a." This is done simply to support the Jehovah's Witnesses' claim that Jesus is not God (Jehovah) and that Jesus is beneath Jehovah and separate from Him. Jehovah's Witnesses acknowledge that "the Word," in John 1:1, is Jesus, but they claim that Jesus was only "a god." John 1:1 is translated *"the Word was God"* in all English Christian Bibles and that translation is supported by all reputable Greek scholars.

We established that we have different understandings of John 1:1 and that I believe Jesus is God and they do not. It was clear this would be the subject of our discussion. I then asked, "why did the Pharisees want Jesus crucified?" They responded, "because He did

JOHN 1:1, 14        HEBREWS 1:8
How to Witness to Jehovah's Witnesses
JOHN 10:30 -
I AND THE FATHER ARE ONE   ACTS 20:28
JOHN 10:33 -     JOHN 20:28 - JESUS DIDN'T CORRECT HIM

things that violated the Law." TITUS 2:13
JOHN 8:58 SAID "I AM"   2 PETER 1:1

I stated it was because they claimed Jesus blasphemed, when Jesus said that He _is_ God. They said Jesus never claimed that, and I gave them verses to support that He did.
REV. 19:10 - ONLY WORSHIP GOD

I then asked, "did Jesus lie when He claimed to be God?" They countered using Old Testament verses to say that Jehovah is One God, not three. I defined the Trinity as One God in three distinct Persons—Father, Son and Holy Spirit. They asked, quoting Deuteronomy 6:4, "why does the Bible say that, 'the Lord our God is One Lord,' if you say He is three persons?" I explained that the Bible is a book of progressive revelation. To the nation of Israel, God revealed Himself as One God. The people of Israel did not understand God to be Father, nor did they know of the Triune God. Before God sent Jesus, He called His people out of the world, and prepared them to be holy and separate unto Himself. He was also preparing them to recognize Jesus as their Messiah. Jesus, during His earthly ministry, revealed more and more about the Godhead and God's plan to redeem mankind. He spoke of God as Father and of the unity He has with the Father and the Spirit. After the Lord's death, burial and resurrection, the New Covenant was fully revealed through the testimony of the apostles; but, prior to the cross, these things were a mystery.

I had already given each man a list of verses that support that Jesus _did_ claim to be God. I keep this list of verses by my front door (The list is included in this book. See "Jesus is God."). I pointed out that, "if Jesus was not God (as they claim), then Jesus lied, which is a sin. And, if Jesus sinned, then His blood was not pure and He could not have paid the price for our sins." They didn't have a response to this.

The Jehovah's Witnesses do NOT believe in Heaven, at least not in the Heaven that the Bible teaches. They believe man will dwell here on a new earth someday, using Isaiah's prophesy of the Millennial Kingdom and the New Heaven and New Earth of Revelation 21 and 22 as support (although they do believe the 144,000 witnesses of Revelation 7 go to Heaven, but we didn't discuss that).

They asked me, "where in the Bible do you read about Heaven?" I referenced Revelation 4 and 5 and described the beauty of the Throne Room, seen and written about by John—the colors, the glassy sea, the One who sits on the throne, who is the Lamb who had been slain, the 24 elders praising Jesus and casting their crowns at His feet, and more. We continued to discuss Heaven and then they quoted John 3:13, *"And no man hath ascended up to heaven, but he that came down from heaven, even the Son of man which is in heaven."*

They asked, "How can you go to Heaven when Jesus said no one can go there?" Again, I reminded them the Bible is a book of progressive revelation and I explained that Jesus spoke those words before He opened the way to Heaven. It is true that before the cross no one could go to Heaven where God dwelt. The payment for sin had to be made. I told them about Luke 16, Abraham's Bosom, the place where all Old Testament saints went at death. I quoted Ephesians 4:8, which tells that Jesus led those in Abraham's Bosom to Heaven when He ascended. Their sins had now been fully paid for, and they were redeemed by the blood of Jesus and given His righteousness. They countered with Matthew 24, saying, "we must persevere to the end," which launched us into a discussion of eschatology, including Matthew 24, Daniel 9 and Revelation 6-22. Of course they didn't agree with most of what I said. The elder understood only part of Daniel 9, failing to understand the unspoken parenthesis that is the church age and the completion of the seventieth week that is yet to be fulfilled.

They asked, "where do you think Adam came from?" I said, "he was created from the dust of the ground, in perfection, to live with God in perfect communion and to have dominion over the earth... but, sadly, he sinned." We agreed on that.

I then asked, "why are we born?" They said "to have dominion over the earth and to work on earth." I countered by saying, "we are born 'for God's pleasure' (Eph 1:5, Rev 4:11), and for His good purposes (Rom 8:28, Eph 1:9, Phil 2:13), and to love, serve and glorify God's name, and to enjoy Him forever." They didn't seem to understand that. I'm not surprised, since the Jehovah's Witnesses is a works-based religion. Their righteousness is earned by what they do, rather than received because of what Christ has done. That's one reason they so actively witness—to make themselves worthy in God's eyes. Somehow we then moved on to Jesus' blood atonement that paid for man's sin.

They agreed that animal blood could not atone for man's sin, and said, "only Jesus' blood could pay the ransom price" ("Not if He lied about being God," I reminded them). This led into a discussion of whether Jesus was fully God and fully man in His incarnation.

They believe Jesus was only a man. They believe Jesus was born of Mary, but not begotten of God. The elder didn't understand begotten, even though it is used in John 3:16 in the NWT. We discussed adoption as children of God and I explained the difference between being an adopted son of God and Jesus being the begotten Son of God (begotten means proceeding from; of the same being). I asked the elder if he has children. He has two biological children, so I commented that they are his begotten children, not his adopted children.

We talked about Jesus' preexistence before His incarnation. Jehovah's Witnesses believe Jesus is a created being (like the angels). In fact, at one point the two men said Jesus _is_ an angel. This comes from the their belief that Jesus was Michael the Archangel before His incarnation and that He became Michael the Archangel again, when He ascended to Heaven 40 days after His resurrection. This makes no sense. In Jude 1:9 Michael the archangel calls upon Jesus to come to his aid. And in Daniel 10:13, Michael is called "one of the chief princes," which means Michael is a higher rank of angel (an archangel), but Michael is still an angel and only one of that rank. Claiming Jesus is "one of the chief princes" (an archangel) denies Scripture. Scripture clearly teaches that Jesus is higher than the angels (read Hebrews 1:1-8 in appendix).

There was much more we talked about, including an illustration I showed them challenging their belief that Jesus is not God (See: "Everything That Exists" in this book). I asked them to please read the printed list of verses that I had given them, even if only to see where we disagree. I later prayed (and still do) that God will reveal truth to them through the verses from His Word.

I then gave them my business card, directed them to the Reasons for Hope website (explaining it is a Christian apologetics ministry) and gave them each a bottle of water (it was a hot day). The elder asked, if he came back with a KJV Bible, could he share some verses with me? I said absolutely...and I hope he does. I care about their souls and they need to know the true Jesus. They need to know that Jesus is God. Their eternal destiny is at stake. They need salvation in Jesus, for without Him they are perishing.

Please say a prayer for Del and Nick. Pray that they will come to know Jesus as the only begotten Son of God. Jesus died for their sins and He desires that they come to Him in true faith, so they can be adopted into God's family, as children of God. Pray that these two men, and all Jehovah's Witnesses, will come to know the One True and Triune God and be blessed to enjoy Him forever.

### What Else Do Jehovah's Witnesses Believe?

Jehovah's Witnesses is also known as the Watchtower Bible and Tract Society, or simply the Watchtower Society. It was founded in 1884 by Charles Taze Russell (1852-1916), and they claim that their doctrines are definitive answers to all questions about Jesus and God. There's a lot of false teaching in the religion of Jehovah's Witnesses, including:

Jehovah's Witnesses believe, with certainty, that they know the exact date of Jesus' birth and the exact year of His death.

Jehovah's Witnesses believe Jesus became the Messiah at His baptism, which is contrary to what the Bible teaches. Jesus was hailed as the prophesied Messiah at His birth (Isa 9:6; Matt 1:16-18; 2:4; Luke 2:11,26).

Jehovah's Witnesses believe Jesus was crucified on a "torture stake," instead of a cross (Matt. 27:32, NWT).

Jehovah's Witnesses believe Jesus returned to earth in 1914, based on their calculations and their claims of knowing His exact birth and death dates. They believe Jesus began His rule as King of God's heavenly government on earth in 1914, but no one has seen Jesus because He does not appear physically on earth.

Jehovah's Witnesses believe that Jesus' resurrection was only spiritual. They do not believe His physical body was resurrected from the grave.

Jehovah's Witnesses believe that, at death, both man's body *and* soul cease to exist. Man remains in this state until the time of the bodily resurrection, when the soul is made alive to live again during the 1,000 year reign of Christ (the Millennium Kingdom).

Jehovah's Witnesses believe that during the Millennium man will be judged by his works, not on his past deeds or sins. Those who do good works will live on after the Millennium and those who have failed in good works will go to Gehenna to be annihilated (no eternal damnation). At one time, Jehovah's Witnesses believed all men would be resurrected in the bodily resurrection, but in 1914 (their false belief that Jesus returned), their doctrine changed.

Having a basic understanding of the false beliefs of Jehovah's Witnesses is helpful in witnessing to them. However, you will never be able to fully understand their beliefs because there is so much that opposes and denies what the Bible teaches.

Understand that there is some truth in what they teach. If that were not the case, very few people would believe anything they teach. Also realize that the errors in their doctrines are subtle...but very significant. Even subtle false teachings are significant heresies.

Before providing you with "Jesus is God" verses and an example to teach the Trinity, I will present a sampling of some of the teachings of the Watchtower Society (indicated by "JW") from www.jw.org.[1] In response to these teachings, I provide Christian doctrine that exposes the errors. All underlining is mine and is provided to emphasize significant errors.

## What is God's name?

JW: The Bible teaches that God has many titles. "God" and "Lord" are among them. However, the Bible also teaches that God has a personal name: Jehovah. Ps 83:18 says: "You, whose name is Jehovah, you alone are the Most High over all the earth."[2]

*Christian doctrine:* Jehovah (Anglicanized form of Yahweh) is the covenantal name of God that He gave to His people Israel (Exodus 3:14). While it is true that this *is* God's name, until God sent His only begotten Son to earth, the people did not know God's triune nature. When God the Father sent His Son, He gave Him the name, Jesus. He is the Christ (in Hebrew: Messiah) and the Lord (supreme God).

*Mat 1:21 And she shall bring forth a son, and thou shalt call his name JESUS: for he shall save his people from their sins.*

*Phil 2:10-11 That at the name of Jesus every knee should bow, of things in heaven, and things in earth, and things under the earth; And that every tongue should confess that Jesus Christ is Lord, to the glory of God the Father.*

## Who is Jesus Christ?

JW: The Bible teaches that Jesus lived in heaven before he came to earth...As a spirit creature in heaven, Jesus had a special relationship with Jehovah...Jesus is Jehovah's most precious Son—and for good reason. He is called "the firstborn of all creation," for he was God's first creation...Jesus is the only one directly created by God. Jesus is also the only one whom God used when He created all other things...Jesus is called "the Word." (John 1:14)

1 http://www.jw.org/
2 http://www.jw.org/en/publications/books/bible-teach/what-is-the-truth-about-god/

This tells us that he spoke for God, no doubt delivering messages and instructions to the Father's other sons, both spirit and human...the Son was created. Obviously, then, he had a beginning, whereas Jehovah God has no beginning or end. (Ps 90:2) [3]

*Christian doctrine:* The New Testament clearly reveals in the words of Jesus, and through the teachings of Paul and other writers, that Jesus is One with the Father and He is God. Jesus said:

*John 10:30 I and my Father are one.*

Jesus was not a "spirit creature" in Heaven, nor was He "God's first creation...the only one directly created by God," as the Jehovah's Witnesses claim. Compare 1 Cor 1:31 and Jer 9:24, 1 Cor 2:16 and Isa 40:13, 1 Cor 10:26 and Ps 24:1, 2 Cor 10:17 and Jer 9:24. In each Old Testament verse "the Lord" is Jehovah. In each New Testament verse, "the Lord" is Jesus. Another example of this is in Romans 10 and Joel 2:

*Rom 10:13 For whosoever shall call upon the name of the Lord shall be saved. [the name of the Lord here is, Jesus]*

*Joel 2:32 And it shall come to pass, that whosoever shall call on the name of the LORD shall be delivered... [the name of the Lord here is, Yahweh/Jehovah]*

Jesus is not called "the Word" because "he spoke for God." Jesus is called "the Word" because *He IS God* and He spoke. Jesus was not created, as Jehovah's Witnesses claim. Just as, "Jehovah God has no beginning or end (Psalm 90:2)," so also Jesus is from eternity past, without beginning or end.

*Micah 5:2 But thou, Bethlehem Ephratah, though thou be little among the thousands of Judah, yet out of thee shall he come forth unto me that is to be ruler in Israel; whose goings forth have been from of old, from everlasting.*

*John 8:58 Jesus said unto them, Verily, verily, I say unto you, Before Abraham was, I am.*

3 http://www.jw.org/en/publications/books/bible-teach/who-is-jesus-christ/

*Rev 1:8 I am Alpha [the first] and Omega [the last], the begin-ning and the ending, saith the Lord, which is, and which was, and which is to come, the Almighty [the Mighty God of whom Isaiah prophesied].*

## Jesus' Pre-existence

JW: Reasonably, then, the archangel Michael is Jesus Christ... So the evidence indicates that the Son of God was known as Michael before he came to earth and is known also by that name since his return to heaven where he resides as the glorified spirit Son of God.[4]

*Christian doctrine:* The idea of Jesus being Michael the Archangel is the foolishness of those who do not know Jesus (1 Corinthians 1:18). It is a false teaching. Read Hebrews 1:1-8 in the Appendix the tell us Jesus is higher than the angels.

## Jesus' Death

Jehovah's Witnesses teach that Jesus had to "buy back what Adam lost" and the doctrine of this purchase is called "The Ransom." This is subtly untrue and an insufficient understanding of Jesus' atoning death.

JW: Jehovah came to mankind's rescue by means of the ransom. What is a ransom? The idea of a ransom basically involves two things. First, a ransom is the price paid to bring about a release or to buy something back. It might be compared to the price paid for the release of a prisoner of war. Second, a ransom is the price that covers, or pays, the cost of something. It is similar to the price paid to cover the damages caused by an injury. For example, if a person causes an accident, he would have to pay an amount that fully corresponds to, or equals, the value of what was damaged. [5]

*Christian doctrine:* There is some truth in this, in that we are ran-somed by Jesus from being slaves to sin and subject to death. How-

4  http://wol.jw.org/
5  Ibid.

ever, Jesus' atonement was much more than a "buy back" of what Adam lost. And the question must be asked, from whom was Jesus buying man back? Even sinful man belongs to God.

*Ps 24:1 A Psalm of David. The earth is the LORD'S, and the fulness thereof; the world, and they that dwell therein.*

Jesus' death must be understood as a payment for the sins of mankind and a propitiation (an atonement) that satisfied the wrath of a just God in judging sin. Jesus paid the price for all mankind's sin and opened the way to eternal life with God (John 14:6). In doing so He ransomed us from being slaves to sin and death.

The Jehovah's Witnesses' inadequate teaching about Jesus' atoning death supports the greater errors in their teachings on salvation and eternal life. They do not believe what Jesus said, "It is finished," or what Paul taught "...by grace are ye saved through faith...Not of works, lest any man should boast." (Ephesians 2:8-9).

## Jesus' Resurrection

JW: It follows that Christ could not take his body back again in the resurrection, thereby taking back the sacrifice offered to God for mankind. Besides, Christ was no longer to abide on earth. His "home" is in the heavens with his Father, who is not flesh, but spirit. (John 14:3; 4:24) Jesus Christ therefore received a glorious immortal, incorruptible body...[6]

*Christian doctrine:* It is correct that Jesus' resurrected body was "a glorious immortal, incorruptible body," but to say that it was because He "could not take His [mortal] body back," for the reason that it would be "taking back the sacrifice offered," is confused reasoning. It was not the death of His body that was the atoning sacrifice. It was His blood, poured-out, that made atonement for man's sins.

*Heb 9:22 And almost all things are by the law purged with blood; and without shedding of blood is no remission.*

6  http://wol.jw.org/

*1 John 1:7 ...the blood of Jesus Christ his Son cleanseth us from all sin.*

It is documented in biblical and secular writings that the tomb was empty. Jesus' earthly body had risen from the grave and He received a glorified body. We cannot fully understand this. His glorified body is similar to, and yet different from, the earthly vessel into which He had been born. Jesus was fully glorified when He ascended to the Father on Sunday morning—glorified in His soul, His spirit and His body of flesh and bones:

*Luke 24:39 Behold my hands and my feet, that it is I myself: handle me, and see; for a spirit hath not flesh and bones, as ye see me have.*

*John 2:19, 21 Jesus answered and said unto them, Destroy this temple, and in three days I will raise it up...he spake of the temple of his body.*

## Judgment Day

JW: In John 12:48 Christ linked the judging of persons with "the last day." Revelation 11:17, 18 locates a judging of the dead as occurring after God takes his great power and begins ruling in a special way as king. [7]

*Christian doctrine:* This completely denies that sin was judged on the cross, paid for by Jesus, and the forgiveness of those sins is received when a repentant sinner trusts in Christ's finished work. This denies that final judgment for eternal life takes place at man's death. It also denies the sufficiency of Christ's death and resurrection to reconcile man to God and give eternal life.

*Heb 9:27 And as it is appointed unto men once to die, but after this [physical death] the judgment [for eternal destiny].*

*Rom 4:25 Who was delivered for our offences [in His atoning death], and was raised again for our justification [salvation].*

---

7  http://wol.jw.org/

## Basis for Judgment

JW: In describing what will take place on earth during the time of judgment, Revelation 20:12 says that the resurrected dead will then be "judged out of those things written in the scrolls according to their deeds." Those resurrected will not be judged on the basis of the works done in their former life, because the rule at Romans 6:7 says: "He who has died has been acquitted from his sin." [8]

*Christian doctrine:* This is so unbiblical, implying that all who die are given a second chance to earn their right standing before God. This claims there is no judgment of man's earthly (pre-Millennial Kingdom) works. Instead it teaches that people will be resurrected and judged according to the works they do when Christ reigns on earth. This is pure works-righteousness and it is heretical.

JW: The resurrected ones will be judged, not on the basis of sin inherited from Adam, but **by what they themselves choose to do**. [in the Millennial Kingdom] Revelation 20:12 says: "The dead were judged out of those things written in the scrolls according to their deeds," that is, their deeds following their resurrection. [9] [emphasis and bracketed information added]

There is so much more false teaching in this system of works righteousness taught by the Jehovah's Witnesses. It is impossible to fully understand because our minds are renewed with the truth of God and so much of their teaching is nonsensical. Spend your time learning God's truths and you will be prepared to answer false claims from any group that is not teaching what the Bible teaches.

We don't want anyone to die in their sins. God desires that all people come to Him (2 Peter 3:9, 1 Timothy 2:6) and that includes Jehovah's Witnesses. Therefore, as Jesus' ambassadors on earth, we need to be prepared to tell all non-believers that Jesus loves them

---

8  http://wol.jw.org/en/wol/d/r1/lp-e/1200002547#h=16
9  http://wol.jw.org/en/wol/d/r1/lp-e/2009200?q=eyes+on+the+prize&p=par#h=11

and offers them saving grace. We need to be prepared, when Jehovah's Witnesses come to our door, to help them "see" the one and only begotten Son of God, the Lord Jesus Christ, the True Light of the World, who is One with the Father

I now provide you with my list of verses that I keep at my front door, as well as an illustration to challenge Jehovah's Witnesses on their false belief that Jesus is not God.

If you would like a copy of the "Jesus is God" verses, email your request to hope@rforh.com. You will be sent a PDF that can be printed and kept near your door. Then, when Jehovah's Witnesses give you their tracts, give them the verses in which Jehovah tells them.... "Jesus IS God."

*Sanctify the Lord God in your hearts: and be ready always to give an answer to every man that asks you a reason of the hope that is in you with meekness and fear [kindness and humbleness].*

*— 1 Peter 3:15*

*In the beginning was the Word, and the Word was with God, and the Word was God. The same was in the beginning with God. All things were made by him; and without him was not any thing made that was made. In him was life; and the life was the light of men.*

*— John 1:1-4*

# Jesus Is God

## The Bible says that Jesus is God

Prophesied in Isaiah and, when the prophesy was fulfilled, Jesus was proclaimed to be God:

*Isa 7:14 Therefore the Lord himself shall give you a sign; Behold, a virgin shall conceive, and bear a son, and shall call his name Immanuel.*

*Mat 1:23 Behold, a virgin shall be with child, and shall bring forth a son, and they shall call his name Emmanuel, which being interpreted is, God with us.*

Jesus was begotten (not made). We are adopted children of God. An adopted child is not a begotten child.

*John 1:14 And the Word was made flesh, and dwelt among us, (and we beheld his glory, the glory as of the only begotten of the Father,) full of grace and truth.*

The English word "begotten" is defined in Hebrew and Greek as:

**Hebrew: 3205. yalad, yaw-lad'**; a prim. root; to bear young; causat. to beget; med. to act as midwife; spec. to show lineage:--bear, beget, birth ([-day]), born, (make to) bring forth (children, young), bring up, calve, child, come, be delivered (of a child), time of delivery, gender, hatch, labour, (do the office of a) midwife, declare pedigrees, be the son of, (woman in, woman that) travail (-eth, -ing woman).

**Greek: 3439. monogenes, mon-og-en-ace'**; from G3441 and G1096; only-born, i.e. sole:--only (begotten, child).

# Jesus said that He is God

God told Moses His name on Mt. Sinai and Jesus claimed that name for Himself:

*Exo 3:14 And God said unto Moses, I AM THAT I AM: and he said, Thus shalt thou say unto the children of Israel, I AM hath sent me unto you.*

*John 8:58 Jesus said unto them, Verily, verily, I say unto you, Before Abraham was, I am.*

*John 10:30 I and my Father are one.*

*John 14:9 Jesus saith unto him, Have I been so long time with you, and yet hast thou not known me, Philip? he that hath seen me hath seen the Father; and how sayest thou then, Show us the Father?*

*John 4:24-26 God is a Spirit: and they that worship him must worship him in spirit and in truth. The woman saith unto him, I know that Messias cometh, which is called Christ: when he is come, he will tell us all things. Jesus saith unto her, I that speak unto thee am he.*

God the Father is Spirit. Jesus the Son took on human flesh when He was incarnated in the womb of Mary.

*Phil 2:7 ... [Jesus] made himself of no reputation, and took upon him the form of a servant, and was made in the likeness of men:*

## Jesus' claim to be God caused the Jews to want to kill Him for blasphemy:

*John 10:31-33 Then the Jews took up stones again to stone him. Jesus answered them, Many good works have I showed you from my Father; for which of those works do ye stone me? The Jews answered him, saying, For a good work we stone thee not; but* **for blasphemy; and because that thou, being a man, makest thyself God.**

The Jews clearly heard and believed that Jesus claimed He is God. IF the response of the Jews was true (Jesus was only "making Himself God") ....then Jesus lied. If Jesus lied, He was not without sin, His blood was not pure and He could not make atonement for man's sin.

## Jesus said that He is the Eternal One

*Isa 9:6  For unto us a child is born [Jesus in human form was born], unto us a son is given [Jesus the Son of God was given]: and the government shall be upon his shoulder: and his name shall be called Wonderful, Counsellor,* **The mighty God, The everlasting Father,** *The Prince of Peace [all names for Jesus].*

*Isa 41:4  Who hath wrought and done it, calling the generations from the beginning?  I the LORD [Jehovah],* **the first, and with the last;** *I am he.*

*Psa 41:13  Blessed be the LORD [Jehovah] God of Israel* **from everlasting, and to everlasting.** *Amen, and Amen.*

*Rev 1:8  **I am Alpha [the first] and Omega [the last], the beginning and the ending,** saith the Lord, which is, and **which was, and which is to come, the Almighty** [the Mighty God of whom Isaiah prophesied].*

*Rev 1:17  And when I [John] saw him, I fell at his feet as dead. And he laid his right hand upon me, saying unto me, Fear not; **I am the first and the last.***

# Only God Deserves Worship

*Mat 4:10 Then saith Jesus unto him, Get thee hence, Satan: for it is written, **Thou shalt worship the Lord thy God, and him only shalt thou serve**.*

**If Jesus were not God, it would have been sinful for Him to accept worship.**

In Matt 8:2, 9:18 and 15:25 Jesus allows people to worship Him and call Him Lord

*Mat 8:2 And, behold, there came a leper and **worshipped him**..*

*Mat 9:18 While he spake these things unto them, behold, there came a certain ruler, and **worshipped him**, saying, My daughter is even now dead: but come and lay thy hand upon her, and she shall live.*

*Mat 15:25 Then came she and **worshipped him**, saying, Lord, help me.*

*Mat 28:9 And as they went to tell his disciples, behold, Jesus met them, saying, All hail. And they came and held him by the feet, and **worshipped him**.*

*John 9:38 And he said, Lord, I believe. And he **worshipped him**.*

# Only God Can Give Eternal Life

*John 4:14 But whosoever drinketh of **the water that I shall give him** shall never thirst; but the water that I shall give him shall be in him **a well of water springing up into everlasting life**.*

*John 5:21 **For as the Father raiseth up the dead, and quickeneth them; even so the Son quickeneth whom he will**.*

*John 10:28  And I [Jesus] give unto them eternal life; and they shall never perish, neither shall any man pluck them out of my hand.*

## Only God has Divine Names

*Psa 23:1  The LORD is my shepherd; I shall not want.*

In John 10:11 & John 10:14 Jesus said; I am the good shepherd…

*Mat 22:42-44  Saying, What think ye of Christ? whose son is he? They say unto him, The son of David. He saith unto them, How then doth David in spirit call him Lord, saying, **The Lord said unto my Lord**, Sit thou on my right hand, till I make thine enemies thy footstool?*

Jesus was quoting Psa 110:1  A Psalm of David. The LORD [Jehovah] said unto my Lord [Adoni- Jesus], Sit thou at my right hand, until I make thine enemies thy footstool. The Scriptures clearly tell Jesus is seated at the right hand of the Father (Heb 1:3, 10:12).

*Isa 43:3  For **I am the LORD thy God, the Holy One of Israel, thy Saviour.**..*

*Luke 1:47  And my [Mary] spirit hath rejoiced in **God [Jesus] my Saviour.**

*Phil 3:20  For our conversation is in heaven; from whence also we look for the Saviour, the Lord Jesus Christ.*

*1 Tim 4:10 …we trust in **the living God, who is the Saviour of all men.**..*

*Psa 27:1  A Psalm of David. **The LORD [Jehovah] is my light** and my salvation; whom shall I fear? the LORD is the strength of my life; of whom shall I be afraid?*

*Micah 7:8  Rejoice not against me, O mine enemy: when I fall, I shall arise; when I sit in darkness,* **the LORD [Jehovah] shall be a light unto me.**

*John 8:12  Then spake Jesus again unto them, saying,* **I am the light of the world***: he that followeth me shall not walk in darkness, but shall have the light of life.*

## Only God is All-knowing & All-powerful

*Mat 8:27  But the men marvelled, saying, What manner of man is this, that even the winds and the sea obey him!*

*Mat 28:18  And Jesus came and spake unto them, saying,* <u>All power is given unto me in heaven and in earth.</u>

*Mat 9:4  And Jesus* <u>knowing their thoughts</u> *said, Wherefore think ye evil in your hearts?*

*Luke 5:22  But when* <u>Jesus perceived their thoughts</u>*, he answering said unto them, What reason ye in your hearts?*

*Luke 6:8  But* <u>he knew their thoughts,</u> *and said to the man which had the withered hand, Rise up, and stand forth in the midst. And he arose and stood forth.*

*Luke 9:47  And Jesus,* <u>perceiving the thought of their heart,</u> *took a child, and set him by him,*

*John 2:24-25  But Jesus did not commit himself unto them, because* <u>he knew all men,</u> *And needed not that any should testify of man: for* <u>he knew what was in man.</u>

*John 4:28-29  The woman then left her waterpot, and went her way into the city, and saith to the men, Come, see* <u>a man, which told me all things that ever I did:</u> *is not this the Christ?*

*John 6:64  But there are some of you that believe not. For <u>Jesus knew from the beginning who they were</u> that believed not, and who should betray him.*

*Acts 1:24  And they prayed, and said, <u>Thou, Lord, which knowest the hearts of all men</u>, show whether of these two thou hast chosen,*

*Col 2:3* **In whom are hid all the treasures of wisdom and knowledge**.

*Col 1:16  For* **by him were all things created**, *that are in heaven, and that are in earth, visible and invisible, whether they be thrones, or dominions, or principalities, or powers: <u>all things were created by him, and for him:</u>*

*Mat 14:25  And in the fourth watch of the night Jesus went unto them, walking on the sea.*

*Luke 8:24  And they came to him, and awoke him, saying, Master, master, we perish. Then he arose, and <u>rebuked the wind and the raging of the water: and they ceased, and there was a calm.</u>*

# Only God Can Forgive Sins

*Mat 9:2, 6 ...Jesus seeing their faith said unto the sick of the palsy; Son, be of good cheer;* **thy sins be forgiven thee**....*that ye may know that* **the Son of man hath power on earth to forgive sins**...

*Mark 2:5, 10  When Jesus saw their faith, he said unto the sick of the palsy,* **Son, thy sins be forgiven thee... the Son of man hath power on earth to forgive sins...**

*Luke 5:24* **...the Son of man hath power upon earth to forgive sins...**

*Luke 7:47,48 ...***Her sins, which are many, are forgiven***...he said unto her,* **Thy sins are forgiven.**

*Acts 5:31  Him [Jesus, the Son] hath God [the Father] exalted with his right hand to be a Prince and a Saviour, for to give repentance to Israel, and* **forgiveness of sins.**

*Col 3:13  Forbearing one another, and forgiving one another, if any man have a quarrel against any: even* **as Christ forgave you,** *so also do ye.*

# Only God is Omnipresent

*Mat 18:20  For* **where two or three are gathered together in my name, there am I** *in the midst of them.*

*Mat 28:20  Teaching them to observe all things whatsoever I have commanded you: and,* **lo, I am with you alway, even unto the end of the world.** *Amen.*

# Jesus said He is the Son of God

*John 9:35-37  Jesus heard that they had cast him out; and when he had found him, he said unto him, Dost thou believe on the Son of God? He answered and said, Who is he, Lord, that I might believe on him? And Jesus said unto him, Thou hast both seen him, and it is he that talketh with thee.*

*If you believe what you like in the Gospel, and reject what you don't like, it is not the Gospel you believe, but yourself.*

— *St. Augustine*

*For by him were all things created, that are in heaven, and that are in earth, visible and invisible, whether they be thrones, or dominions, or principalities, or powers: all things were created by him, and for him:*

*— Colossians 1:16*

# Everything That Exists

These two boxes represent "Everything That Exists." Everything falls into one of the two boxes: That which has always existed and that which has come into existence.

## Everything That Exists

| That which has always existed. | That which has come into existence. |
| --- | --- |

Ask: **"Where do you put God?"**
Answer: **"In the 'That which has always existed' box."**

God has always existed, so He's in the box on the left.


Ask: **"Where do you put all created things?"**
Answer: **"In the 'That which has come into existence' box."**

All created things have come into existence, so they are in the box on the right.

# Everything That Exists

| That which has always existed. GOD | That which has come into existence. All Created Things |
|---|---|

Next ask, **"In which box do you put Jesus?"**

Jehovah's Witnesses will not put Jesus in the left box, because they deny that Jesus is God and they believe that Jesus was created by God. They will want to put Jesus in the box of "That which has come into existence/All Created Things," but ask them to read John 1:3 in the KJV:

*All things were made by him [Jesus]; and without him was not any thing made that was made.*

John 1:3 tells that Jesus made all things, so He can't be in the "All Created Things" box. Jesus did not make Himself. Share this verse:

*Colossians 1:16  For <u>by him [Jesus] were all things created</u>, that are in heaven, and that are in earth, visible and invisible, whether they be thrones, or dominions, or principalities, or powers: <u>all things were created by him</u>, and for him.*

Since Jesus can't be in the "All Created Things" box, Jehovah's Witnesses will try to put Him outside the boxes.  BUT....**there is no "outside the boxes."**  The two boxes represent "Everything That Exists."  Because Jesus exists, they have to put Jesus inside one of the two boxes.

NOTE: Always use the King James Bible. Do not let Jehovah's Witnesses use the New World Translation. The NWT is exclusive to their faith and it is not an accurate translation of ancient manuscripts (see appendix for information on the NWT). Kindly remind them that we have the KJV in common. Both religions trust the words of the KJV and therefore it should be the Bible used.

This is important because when you share John 1:3 with Jehovah's Witnesses they will try to use the false translation of John 1:4 in the NWT to confuse and contradict what John 1:3 teaches.

Remember, your argument is based on John 1:3 *All things were made by him; and without him was not any thing made that was made.*

Now read John 1:4 in both translations and note how the NWT changes this verse:

*(KJV) John 1:4 **In him was life**; and the life was the light of men.*

(NWT) John 1:4 **What has come into existence by means of him was life,** and the life was the light of men.

Jehovah's Witnesses will want you to read John 1:4 in the NWT to support their false teaching that God created Jesus and then Jesus created life. This makes life outside-of and separate-from Jesus, rather than "in Him" (KJV). It also teaches that the "light of men" is the life Jesus created, not the life that is "in Him."

Ancient biblical manuscripts do not support the NWT changes in John 1:4. Use only the King James Bible. It is time proven to be accurate and trustworthy; and until the middle of the 20th century it was the only Bible the Jehovah's Witnesses used.

**FINALLY:** Show the Jehovah's witnesses where to put Jesus.

# Everything That Exists

| That which has always existed. | That which has come into existence. |
|---|---|
| **God the Father** <br> **God the Son** <br> **God the Holy Spirit** | **All Created Things** |

Jesus has always existed because Jesus IS God. That is the biggest stumbling block for Jehovah's Witnesses. They do not know the true Jesus.

Jehovah's Witnesses (The Watchtower Society) is a works-based religion, not a cross-centered relationship. Pray for Jehovah's Witnesses. They have been deceived into believing a lie.

<*}}}><

# Confidence

Before and after any witness encounter, always pray, knowing and trusting that it is God who gives you the strength to share His Word and He is the One who enables you to do so with kindness. Trusting God to empower you will instill confidence in you. Remember also to pray as you are witnessing. It only takes a second to ask, "Lord help me."

*1 John 5:14 Now this is the confidence that we have in Him, that if we ask anything according to His will, He hears us.*

Confidence is an important element in witnessing and it only comes from trusting that the Lord will equip and enable us to share His Word. Let these verses be assurance of the blessings and hope that we have in Jesus as they strengthen our confidence in Him.

*Jer 17:7 "Blessed is the man who in the LORD, And whose hope is the LORD.*

*Psa 71:5 For You are my hope, O Lord GOD; You are my trust from my youth.*

*Heb 6:19 Which hope we have as an anchor of the soul...*

*Prov 3:26 For the LORD will be your confidence, And will keep your foot from being caught.*

*Prov 16:20 He who heeds the word wisely will find good, And whoever trusts in the LORD, happy is he.*

*Prov 14:26 In the fear of the LORD there is strong confidence*

*Phil 1:6 being confident of this very thing, that He who has begun a good work in you will complete it until the day of Jesus Christ.*

Stand on the confidence you have in the Lord and be bold as you speak His truths. Be prepared and ready to give reasons for your hope, with kindness and humbleness. Tell people who Jesus is, what He has done for them and how they can know Him. Tell them that Jesus loves them and offers them the riches of the glory of His forgiveness and His saving grace.

*John 3:16 For God so loved the world, that he gave his only begotten Son, that whosoever believeth in him should not perish, but have everlasting life.*

*1 Pet 3:15 But sanctify the Lord God in your hearts, and always be ready to give a defense to everyone who asks you a reason for the hope that is in you, with meekness and fear.*

The Comforter, which is the Holy Ghost, whom the Father will send in my name, he shall teach you all things, and bring all things to your remembrance, whatsoever I have said unto you.

— John 14:26

**THEY RECEIVED THE WORD**
*with all readiness of mind and*
**SEARCHED THE SCRIPTURES**
*daily to find out whether
these things were so.*
ACTS 17:11

# The New World Translation

When I was in bank management, we trained tellers to spot counterfeit bills by giving them genuine U.S. currency to study. They learned exactly what each bill looked like. They were also given a few counterfeit bills, but did not spend much time studying those. It is impossible to know all the minute differences in counterfeit bills. It is much easier, and more productive, to study an authentic bill and be so familiar with it that a counterfeit stands out as being "off the mark." The same is true of false religions.

I do not recommend reading the New World Translation (NWT). Our time is much better spent reading God's Word. When we are well equipped with the truths of the Christian Bible, only a general understanding of the history of the NWT and its corruption of some verses is necessary. The next few pages will equip you with some additional information and a basic knowledge about the NWT and how the Jehovah's Witnesses use it to support their unbiblical doctrines.

### A Brief History of the New World Translation

The New Testament of the NWT was published in 1950 by the Watchtower Bible and Tract Society. The Old Testament was released in five separate volumes from 1953-1960. The complete NWT was released in 1961. Since that time, the NWT has been revised four times.

Prior to 1961, Jehovah's Witnesses used the King James Version of the Bible. While they still recognize the KJV as acceptable, Jehovah's Witnesses believe the NWT is of greater accuracy on many passages, and they teach that the NWT is authoritative.

The primary translator of the NWT was Frederick Franz, a liberal arts major from the University of Cincinnati with only two years of biblical languages study. Franz later became President of the Watchtower Bible and Tract Society and served from 1977-1992.

### Additions and Errors

The New World Translation is inconsistent with all reputable Christian Bible translations. The following verses will show how the NWT alters verses in attempts to support false doctrines.

My purpose in sharing these is to make you aware of how Jehovah's Witnesses twist Scripture and to show why I recommend you only discuss verses using the King James translation. Do not let Jehovah's Witnesses use the NWT. They will confuse you with the subtle differences that make it a heretical document. Remember, up until 1950 they only used the KJV. Since the KJV is common to both Christianity and Jehovah's Witnesses, it is not unreasonable to insist that it be the Bible used in your conversation. If you are not familiar with the KJV, do not be concerned. The verses will be consistent with whatever translation you read, and you can trust that it is the Word of God. The NWT is *not* the Word of God. It contains man's words.

In comparing the KJV and NWT, please note that for the NWT I am providing verses from both the 1984 and 2013 editions. These are not reprints. They are revisions with many changes.

In all English Bible translations there are added words, which are not found in the original language manuscripts. Many are added because a word in the original language does not have a direct translation into English. Some are simply for reading-flow in the English language. The KJV and other Bibles place these words in brackets or italics to inform the reader of the additions.

Take note that added words in the 1984 NWT are bracketed. Note also that the brackets have been deleted in the 2013 NWT revision for many of the added words. By removing the brackets, the 2013 revision does not indicate to the reader which words have been added. Removing the brackets also implies that the words were present in the original language manuscripts, thereby making them authoritative. This is significant, because many of the previously bracketed words were added to deny the deity of Jesus.

Note also in these comparisons that some text is underlined. The underlining is mine. I have added it to call your attention to the variations between the two translations.

Understand that the KJV does not capitalize personal pronouns in reference to God. In literary work it is correct *not* to capitalize personal pronouns. However, in recent years many Bible translations have added capitalization to aid the reader in identifying the pronouns that refer to God.

The KJV verses are placed in italics simply to set-apart God's Word from NWT text. Remember, the KJV is the Word of God, and the NWT is not.

### Genesis 1:1-2

(NWT, 1984) In [the] beginning God created the heavens and the earth. Now the earth proved to be formless and waste and there was darkness upon the surface of [the] watery deep; and God's active force was moving to and fro over the surface of the waters.

(NWT, 2013) In the beginning God created the heavens and the earth. Now the earth was formless and desolate, and there was darkness upon the surface of the watery deep, and God's active force was moving about over the surface of the waters.

*(KJV) In the beginning God created the heaven and the earth. And the earth was without form, and void; and darkness [was] upon the face of the deep. And the Spirit of God moved upon the face of the waters.*

Jehovah's Witnesses reject the doctrine of the Trinity, claiming Jesus is NOT God and the Holy Spirit is NOT God. They believe the Holy Spirit is not a person, claiming He is only an extension of Jehovah or an "active force" sent out. The NWT does not capitalize references to the Holy Spirit. This is another way Jehovah's Witnesses try to support their teaching that the Holy Spirit is only a force, not a Person of the Godhead. In Genesis 1:1-2, the NWT translates the Hebrew words "ruwach elohim" as "God's active force" instead of the proven accurate translation of "Spirit of God." Although "ruwach" can be translated as "wind," when used in context with God it is always a reference to the Spirit of God.

### Micah 5:2

(NWT, 1984) And you, O Bethlehem Ephrathah, the one too little to get to be among the thousands of Judah, from you there will come out to me the one who is to become ruler in Israel, whose origin is from early times, from the days of time indefinite.

(NWT, 2013) And you, O Bethlehem Ephrathah, The one too little to be among the thousands of Judah, From you will come out for me the one to be ruler in Israel, Whose origin is from ancient times, from the days of long ago.

*(KJV) But thou, Bethlehem Ephratah, though thou be little among the thousands of Judah, yet out of thee shall he come forth unto me that is to be ruler in Israel; whose goings forth have been from of old, from everlasting.*

What a precious verse this is, for it prophesies of the incarnation of the Lord Jesus Christ. The NWT makes subtle, but significant, changes in Micah 5:2, attempting to support the heresy that Jesus was created.

The NWT presents an "origin" for Jesus by saying: "...whose origin is from early/ancient times..." The KJV says that Jesus' "goings forth have been from old..." This isn't speaking of Jesus having an origin. It's speaking of Jesus existing before He came "out of thee [Bethlehem]." The NWT's use of the word "origin" is wrong, because Jesus had no "origin." Jesus has always existed. He is eternal, without beginning or end.

The NWT also tries to subtly insert an "origin" date for Jesus:

(NWT, 1984) "whose origin is from early times, from the days of time indefinite."

(NWT, 2013) "Whose origin is from ancient times, from the days of long ago."

Both the 1984 and 2013 NWT date an origin for Jesus that is within our time dimension (early times/ancient times). The KJV tells us that Jesus is the Eternal God, when it declares His "goings forth have been from old" (before His incarnation in Bethlehem). The KJV further clarifies this by declaring, "from everlasting." It's easy to see the intent of the Jehovah's Witnesses to deny the deity of Jesus in this verse and to support their claim that Jesus was created by God.

### Zechariah 12:10

(NWT, 1984) And I will pour out upon the house of David and upon the inhabitants of Jerusalem the spirit of favor and entreaties, and they will certainly look to the One whom they pierced through, and they will certainly wail over Him as in the wailing over an only [son]; and there will be a bitter lamentation over him as when there is bitter lamentation over the firstborn [son].

(NWT, 2013) "I will pour out on the house of David and on the inhabitants of Jerusalem the spirit of favor and supplication, and they will look to the one whom they pierced, and they will wail over him as they would wail over an only son; and they will grieve bitterly over him as they would grieve over a firstborn son.

(KJV) And I will pour upon the house of David, and upon the inhabitants of Jerusalem, the spirit of grace and of supplications: and they shall look upon me whom they have pierced, and they shall mourn for him, as one mourneth for his only son, and shall be in bitterness for him, as one that is in bitterness for his firstborn.

Jehovah's Witnesses will agree that this is God (Jehovah) speaking (it's clear in Zechariah 12:1). Since God is speaking in the first person about Himself being pierced through (in KJV), the NWT changes "shall look upon me" to read "shall look to the One" (1984). Then, in the 2013 revision, they have omitted the capitalization so it reads, "shall look to the one." Such changes are intentional, to deny the deity of Jesus, and they are not supported by Hebrew language scholars.

### Mathew 14:33

(NWT, 1984, 2013) Then those in the boat <u>did obeisance to him</u>, saying: "You are really God's Son."

*(KJV) Then they that were in the ship came and <u>worshiped him</u>, saying, Of a truth thou art the Son of God.*

Many people worshiped Jesus, and Jesus accepted their worship (see "Only God Deserves Worship" in "Jesus is God" section of this book).

In order to deny the deity of Jesus, the NWT translates this as "did obeisance" instead of "worshiped him." The Greek word is "proskuneo," which is defined by Strong's Dictionary as to "prostrate oneself in homage (do reverence to, adore)--worship." When the word is used as an action directed to God (Jehovah) the NWT translates this word as "worship" (e.g. John 4:20), but in every case where it is directed to Jesus the NWT uses "obeisance." Obeisance can convey a meaning less than worship. It can mean respect, honor or deference. The word is used to support the heresy that Jesus in not God and therefore He was not worshiped, nor did He accept worship.

### Luke 23:20-21

(NWT, 1984) Again Pilate called out to them, because he wanted to release Jesus. Then they began to yell, saying: <u>"Impale! Impale him!"</u>

(NWT, 2013) Again Pilate called out to them, because he wanted to release Jesus. Then they began to yell, saying: "To the stake with him! To the stake with him!"

*(KJV) Pilate therefore, willing to release Jesus, spake again to them. But they cried, saying, Crucify him, crucify him.*

Jehovah's Witnesses claim that Jesus was not crucified on a cross, but instead was impaled on a stake. The NWT calls the cross a "torture stake" in both Matthew 10:38 and 27:32. The Greek word used in those verses is "stauros." Strong's Dictionary defines "stauros" as "a stake or post (as set upright), i.e. (spec.) a pole or cross (as an instrument of capital punishment)." Since the word can mean both "stake" and "cross," there must be other considerations to determine which translation is correct. There is much evidence to support that "cross" is the correct translation.

In addition to ancient biblical and secular documents that recorded Jesus' crucifixion, there was also oral history that spoke of Jesus being crucified on a cross. The oral history of that time was passed-down, just as the written documents were. Ancient historical documents clearly declare that Jesus was crucified, not impaled. It is also a well documented fact that a cross was used for capital punishment by the Romans and that Jesus was nailed to the cross through His hands and feet. There is nothing to support the Jehovah's Witnesses' idea that Jesus' hands were positioned above His head, overlapping as His feet were, and He was pierced through both hands with only one nail (this is illustrated in drawings from the Watchtower Society).

It should be noted that the fourth century Latin Vulgate translates "stauros" as "crucem," which translates in English to "cross." Note also that all early English Bibles translate "stauros" as "cross." Changing the word from "cross" to "stake" (and the word "crucify" to "impale") is yet another attempt by Jehovah's Witnesses to deny the validity of Christian Bibles and to encourage people to consider a different view of Jesus' death. Perhaps the underlying intention is to create doubts about other truths in the Christian Bible, especially the Bible's declaration that Jesus is God.

## John 1:1

(NWT, 1984)  In [the] beginning the Word was, and the Word was with God, and the Word was a god.

(NWT, 2013) In the beginning was the Word, and the Word was with God, and the Word was a god.

*(KJV) In the beginning was the Word, and the Word was with God, and the Word was God.*

We've looked at this verse, but it merits further discussion. Two Greek words are used in this verse: logos and theos. Every legitimate Christian Bible translation reads, "the Word [logos] was God [theos]." The NWT adds the indefinite article, "a," to support their heresy that Jesus is not Jehovah God. The phrase in the Greek language includes a definite article, "ho," and reads, "theos en ho logos." The Watchtower Society claims the "ho" is an indefinite description that should precede "theos" and, since it follows "theos," an "a" should be added before "theos." This theory is *not* supported by Greek scholars and the addition of "a" before God (theos) is simply another strategy to claim that Jesus is not God.

## Acts 20:28

(NWT, 1984)  Pay attention to yourselves and to all the flock, among which the holy spirit has appointed YOU overseers, to shepherd the congregation of God, which he purchased with the blood of his own [Son].

(NWT, 2013) Pay attention to yourselves and to all the flock, among which the holy spirit has appointed you overseers, to shepherd the congregation of God, which he purchased with the blood of his own Son.

*(KJV) Take heed therefore unto yourselves, and to all the flock, over the which the Holy Ghost hath made you overseers, to feed the church of God, which he hath purchased with his own blood.*

Only the NWT adds [Son] to this verse. "Son" is not found in any

Greek manuscripts. This verse is clearly trinitarian, stating that God ransomed man with "his own blood." Since there is no dispute it was Jesus who died on the cross, this verse states that Jesus and God are One...therefore Jesus IS God. Jehovah's Witnesses changed this verse to deny that truth. Note the brackets around "Son" were removed in the 2013 revision, implying this is from the original manuscripts. The NWT also records the name of the Holy Spirit in lower case letters to support their claim that He is not God, but only an "active force" of God.

### Colossians 1:16,17

(NWT, 1984) because by means of him all [other] things were created in the heavens and upon the earth, the things visible and the things invisible, no matter whether they are thrones or lordships or governments or authorities. All [other] things have been created through him and for him. Also, he is before all [other] things and by means of him all [other] things were made to exist,

(NWT, 2013) because by means of him all other things were created in the heavens and on the earth, the things visible and the things invisible, whether they are thrones or lordships or governments or authorities. All other things have been created through him and for him. Also, he is before all other things, and by means of him all other things were made to exist,

*(KJV) For by him were all things created, that are in heaven, and that are in earth, visible and invisible, whether [they be] thrones, or dominions, or principalities, or powers: all things were created by him, and for him: And he is before all things, and by him all things consist.*

Again in this verse, the NWT inserts a word. The word, "other" is added to deny the deity of Jesus and to claim that Jesus was the first of God's creation. Jehovah's Witnesses claim that after Jesus was created, He then created all "other" things. The word "other" is not found in the original Greek manuscripts. Note also that "other" was bracketed in 1984, but the deception increases with the removal of brackets in the 2013 revision. The KJV is correct in saying that *ALL things were created by Jesus*, because Jesus is God. Denying this truth is the underlying blindness and stumbling block for Jehovah's Witnesses and leads to their false teachings in the New World Translation.

### Titus 2:13

(NWT, 1984) while we wait for the happy hope and glorious manifestation of the great God and of [the] Savior of us, Christ Jesus.

(NWT, 2013) while we wait for the happy hope and glorious manifestation of the great God and of our Savior, Jesus Christ

*(KJV) Looking for that blessed hope, and the glorious appearing of the great God and our Saviour Jesus Christ.*

Jehovah's Witnesses twist this verse by changing the words. The KJV uses "blessed hope" and the NWT changes this to "happy hope." "Blessed Hope" is a title for Jesus. He is our Blessed Hope and we are to be "looking for" Him, who the verse proclaims to be "the great God and our Saviour." This is referencing Jesus' return for His church. Jehovah's Witnesses insert the word "of" (without brackets) to influence readers to think that this is referring to God (Jehovah) and Jesus as separate. However, this verse is speaking of Jesus alone, as "the great God *and* our Saviour." God the Father is spirit and He will not be "appearing." We are to be looking for Jesus who is one with God the Father and is *both* our great God and Saviour.

Notice also how the NWT's changes "Savior of us, Christ Jesus" (1984) to "our Savior, Jesus Christ" (2013). "Christ Jesus" puts the emphasis on Jesus' divinity and "Jesus Christ" puts emphasis on His humanity. It's simply another attempt to deny that Jesus is God.

Spend your time studying God's Word. Your knowledge of the truth found in the Holy Bible will equip you to spot errors in the false teachings of all counterfeit religions. Be prepared with a basic knowledge of what Jehovah's Witnesses believe and what they will present when they come to your door.

Print out some verses and be ready to challenge Jehovah's Witnesses to understand that Jesus IS God. When they give you their tract from the Watchtower Society, give them God's words from the Holy Bible. And, of course...pray for them. They need God to open their ears so they can hear, and soften their hearts so they will repent. They need to turn to the true Jesus in faith, knowing that Jesus IS God and trusting in His work alone to save their souls.

<*}}}><

*Study to show thyself approved unto God, a workman that needeth not to be ashamed, rightly dividing the word of truth.*

— *2 Timothy 2:15*

for there are three
that bear record
in heaven,

the **Father**

the **Word**

the **Holy Ghost**

and these three are one.
1 John 5:7

# Appendix

# Understanding the Trinity

Because the Jehovah's Witnesses deny that Jesus is God, they do not believe in a triune God. Therefore, in talking with Jehovah's Witnesses, it is import to understand the biblical Doctrine of the Trinity and be able to share verses that support it.

It is difficult for our finite human brains to fully conceive of an infinite being, but God's Word gives us everything we need to come to a sufficient understanding of the nature of God as triune.

The Bible teaches that the Father is God, Jesus is God, and the Holy Spirit is God—and that there is only one God. Each Person of the Trinity is distinct in Himself. We often simply state this as: The Trinity is one God, existing in three Persons. Remember, this does not mean three Gods. It means three distinct Persons, who are ONE God. This is not easy to comprehend, but it is true and it is a core Christian doctrine that can be understood.

Jehovah's Witnesses challenge the triunity of God by claiming that the word "trinity" is not found in Scripture. While that is true, the word is not there, neither is the word "Bible" found in the Bible, or the words, rapture, incarnation, atheism, or even monotheism (meaning One God). While those words are not found in the Bible, the foundational teaching for each word is clearly presented in Scripture.

Be prepared to show Jehovah's Witnesses verses that support the understanding that God is One God in three distinct Persons. The Father, Son and Holy Spirit are coexistent, co-eternal and co-equal.

## There is One God

*Deut 6:4  Hear, O Israel: The LORD our God is one LORD...*

*1 Cor 8:4  ...we know that an idol is nothing in the world, and that there is none other God but one.*

*Gal 3:20  Now a mediator is not a mediator of one, but God is one.*

*1 Tim 2:5  For there is one God, and one mediator between God and men, the man Christ Jesus...*

## The Trinity Consists of Three Persons

*Gen 1:1  In the beginning God created the heaven and the earth.*
[The Hebrew word for God in Gen 1:1 is Elohim, a plural word.]

*Gen 1:26  And God said, Let us make man in our image, after our likeness...*

*Gen 3:22  And the LORD God said, Behold, the man is become as one of us, to know good and evil...*

*Gen 11:7  Go to, let us go down...*

*Isa 6:8  Also I heard the voice of the Lord, saying, Whom shall I send, and who will go for us?*

*Matt 3:16-17  And Jesus, when he was baptized, went up straightway out of the water: and, lo, the heavens were opened unto him, and he saw the Spirit of God descending like a dove, and lighting upon him: And lo a voice from heaven, saying, This is my beloved Son, in whom I am well pleased.*  [In this verse we see the presence of all three Persons of the Trinity: the Son, Jesus, the Spirit descending and the Father speaking]

*Matt 28:19  Go ye therefore, and teach all nations, baptizing them in the name of the Father, and of the Son, and of the Holy Ghost.*
[Only one name, but three Persons]

*2 Cor 13:14 The grace of the Lord Jesus Christ, and the love of God, and the communion of the Holy Ghost, be with you all. Amen.* [Again we read of all three Persons of the Trinity]

*1 John 5:7 For there are three that bear record in heaven, the Father, the Word, and the Holy Ghost: and these three are one.*

## Each Person of the Trinity is God

### The Father is God.

*Rom 1:7 ...Grace to you and peace from God our Father, and the Lord Jesus Christ.*

*1 Pet 1:3 Blessed be the God and Father of our Lord Jesus Christ...*

### The Son is God.

*John 1:1 In the beginning was the Word, and the Word was with God, and the Word was God.*

*John 1:14 And the Word was made flesh, and dwelt among us, (and we beheld his glory, the glory as of the only begotten of the Father,) full of grace and truth.*

*Rom 9:5 ...Christ came, who is over all, God blessed for ever. Amen*

*Col 2:9 For in him dwelleth all the fulness of the Godhead bodily.*

*Heb 1:8 But unto the Son he saith, Thy throne, O God, is for ever and ever: a sceptre of righteousness is the sceptre of thy kingdom.*

*1 John 5:20 And we know that the Son of God is come, and hath given us an understanding, that we may know him that is true, and we are in him that is true, even in his Son Jesus Christ. This is the true God, and eternal life.*

### The Holy Spirit is God.

*Acts 5:3 But Peter said, Ananias, why hath Satan filled thine heart to lie to the Holy Ghost, and to keep back part of the price of the land?*

*Acts 5:4 Whiles it remained, was it not thine own? and after it was sold, was it not in thine own power? why hast thou conceived this thing in thine heart? thou hast not lied unto men, but unto God.*

*1 Cor 3:16 Know ye not that ye are the temple of God, and that the Spirit of God dwelleth in you?*

### Three Distinct Persons

There is a pattern of subordination within the Trinity, regarding order, but not in substance or essence. The Son is subordinate to the Father (Luke 22:42, John 5:36, John 20:21, 1 John 4:14); and the Holy Spirit is subordinate to the Son and the Father (John 14:16, John 14:26, John 15:26, John 16:7, 13-14). We need to be careful to understand this subordination in terms of their work, not their Persons, power or position.

Simply put, the three Persons of the Trinity are equal in nature and one in being, but are distinct in Person and distinguishable in their works. Jesus' words reveal His subordination to the Father in His surrender to the will of the Father, to do the work of the Father:

*John 17:4 I have glorified thee on the earth: I have finished the work which thou gavest me to do.*

The Spirit is subordinate to the will of the Father and Son in His work:

*John 16:7 Nevertheless I tell you the truth; It is expedient for you that I go away: for if I go not away, the Comforter will not come unto you; but if I depart, I will send him unto you.*

*John 16:13-14 Howbeit when he, the Spirit of truth, is come, he will guide you into all truth: for he shall not speak of himself; but whatsoever he shall hear, that shall he speak: and he will show you things to come. He shall glorify me: for he shall receive of mine, and shall show it unto you.*

Yes, the Trinity is a difficult doctrine to understand. While it can never be fully comprehended it can be sufficiently understood by studying God's Word, and can be clearly explained to Jehovah's Witness and other non-believers. It is then up to the person, whether they have "ears to hear." Pray that God will open their ears and soften their hearts to receive His words and recognize Jesus as God.

## Illustrating the Trinity

There are many illustrations to explain the Trinity being three in one. Some will reference water, which has three states of solid (frozen), liquid and gas. There's also an apple that has a seed, the "meat" of the apple and the skin; and an egg, with the shell, the white and the yolk. While these give an understanding of three parts, they do not convey the coexistence of the Trinity. A glass of water cannot be solid, liquid and gas at the same time. A skinless apple is still an apple. And an egg without a shell is still an egg.

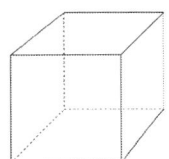 A much better illustration is a cube. A cube has height, width and depth, and all three are required for it to be a cube. If one of those dimensions is removed, it ceases to be a cube.

Understand that whatever illustration we use, it will always fall short. We can never fully explain or illustrate God because He is infinite, outside our space and time dimensions, and He is also omniscient (all knowing). We are constrained by finite space, time and understanding.

The best verse in the Bible that identifies each Person of the Trinity as distinct and yet all three Persons as One God is:

*1 John 5:7 For there are three that bear record in heaven, <u>the Father</u>, <u>the Word</u>, and <u>the Holy Ghost</u>: and **these three are one**.*

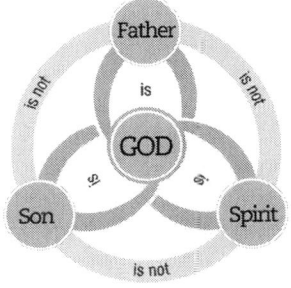

# Appendix

# Hebrews 1:1-8
## Jesus is Higher than the Angels

*[1] God, who at various times and in various ways spoke in time past to the fathers by the prophets, [2] has in these last days spoken to us by His Son, whom He has appointed heir of all things, through whom also He made the worlds; [3] who being the brightness of His glory and the express image of His person, and upholding all things by the word of His power, when He had by Himself purged our sins, sat down at the right hand of the Majesty on high, [4] having become so much better than the angels, as He has by inheritance obtained a more excellent name than they.*

*[5] For to which of the angels did He ever say: "You are My Son, Today I have begotten You"? And again: "I will be to Him a Father, And He shall be to Me a Son"? [6] But when He again brings the firstborn into the world, He says: "Let all the angels of God worship Him." [7] And of the angels He says: "Who makes His angels spirits And His ministers a flame of fire." [8] But to the Son He says: "Your throne, O God, is forever and ever; A scepter of righteousness is the scepter of Your Kingdom.*

FOLLOW ME
I WILL
MAKE YOU Fishers
OF MEN <*}}}><

Matthew 4:19

# Notes and Names

Use these pages to record witnessing experiences and the names of those who need your prayers.

# Notes and Names

# More Books and Resources from the Author

*Why the Butterfly? Rightly Remembering Jesus*, by Shari Abbott. This book isn't about butterflies. . .it's all about Jesus! Discover how rightly remembering will establish your heart, anchor your soul and transform your mind. A quick read that will give you a heavenly perspective on this journey we call life!

*Remember Me - A Course In Rightly Remembering* A video study that teach rightly remembering and ignites a desire to filter everything we think, say and do through the hope that is found in Jesus Christ.

*Who Said That? Common everyday sayings...where do they come from?* by Shari Abbott. This is a great book to give unbelievers. It presents everyday sayings that originate from God's Word. At the end of the book is a gospel presentation.

*Fun with "Shuns"* Learn key doctrines of the Christian faith by understanding the many words in the Bible that end in -tion. Includes five short videos. If you can't fully explain why you believe what you believe, then you need this book. DVD and book for group or individual study. Also available as iBook with video.

*Got Questions? We have Reasons for Hope, Reasons Books 1 & 2,* by Shari Abbott. Real questions from real people. Each book has 30 questions and biblical answers with reasons for hope.

*How to Witness to Jehovah's Witnesses, Apologetics Answers & Verses,* by Shari Abbott. Be prepared to defend what you believe and be able to present biblical truth the next time a Jehovah's Witness comes to your door. Don't be out-witnessed by a Jehovah's Witness.

## Visit www.rforh.com/store

*Preach the word!*
*Be ready in season and out of season.*
*— 2 Timothy 4:2*

# *reasonsforhope**

## *Jesus

Reasons for Hope exists to offset the hopelessness that is prevalent in our time and culture and to direct people to the biblical Jesus.

**H**elping Christians share the Gospel of Jesus Christ.

**O**ffsetting secular thinking with biblical truth.

**P**roviding resources that give biblical answers to real-world questions.

**E**ncouraging Christians to rely on God's Word as the foundation for their thoughts, their words and their actions.

Any questions, email us at questions@rforh.com.

Share your thoughts — email hope@rforh.com

Connect with us:
  Facebook: /reasonsforhope | Twitter: @reasons4hope
  Sign up to get apologetics teachings via email: www.rforh.com